RECORDED VERSIONS
GUITAR

AUTHENTIC TRANSCRIPTIONS
WITH NOTES AND TABLATURE

**Transcribed by
JESSE GRESS**

THE • BEATLES
REVOLVER

GW01045285

ISBN 0-7935-2622-1

HAL•LEONARD
CORPORATION

7777 W. BLUEMOUND RD. P.O. BOX 13819 MILWAUKEE, WI 53213

This publication is not for sale in
the E.C. and/or Australia
or New Zealand.

And Your Bird Can Sing

Words and Music by John Lennon and Paul McCartney

MCA music publishing

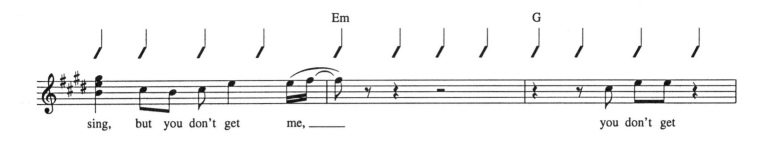

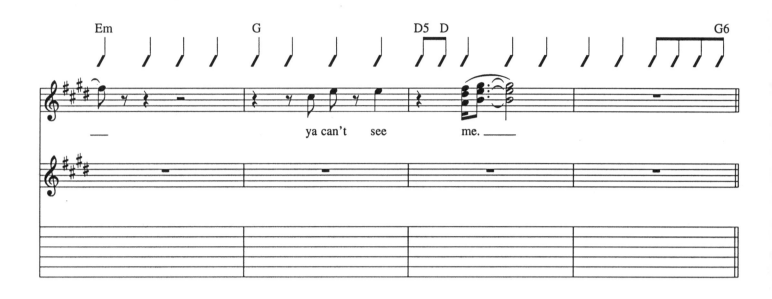

ya can't see me.

Bridge

when your prized po - ses - sions start to weigh you down,

Gtr. 1 w/semi-dist.

let ring

look in my di - rec - tion, I'll be 'round, I'll be 'round.

let ring

let ring

Guitar Solo

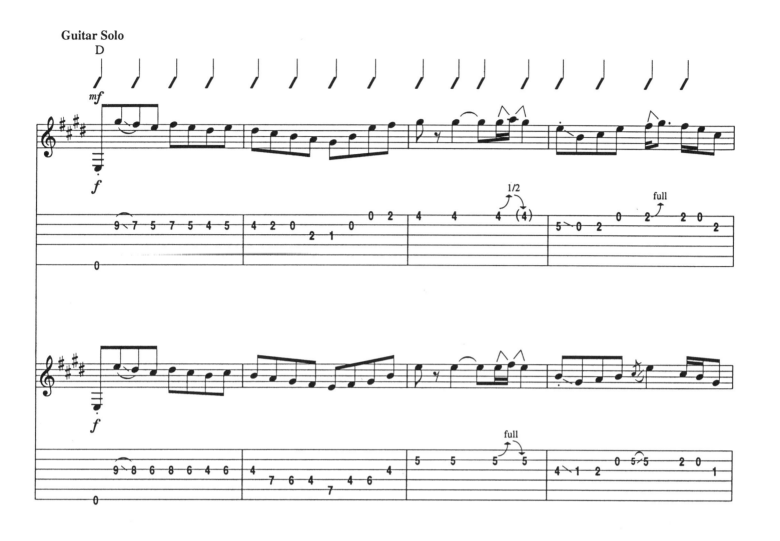

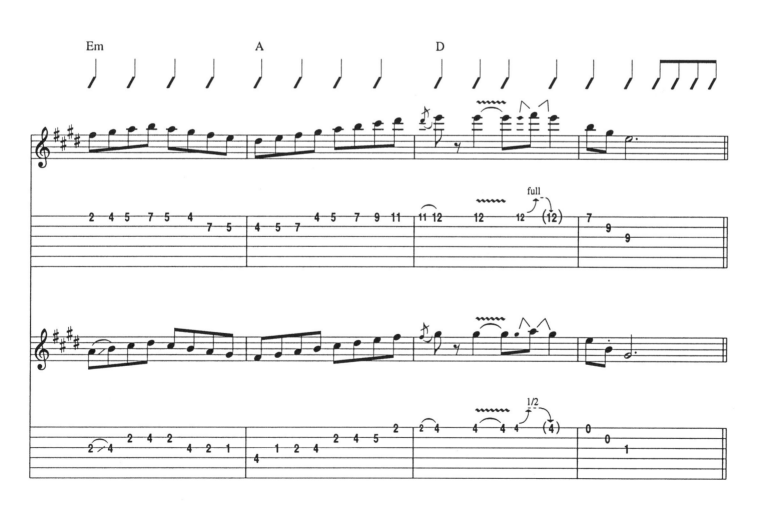

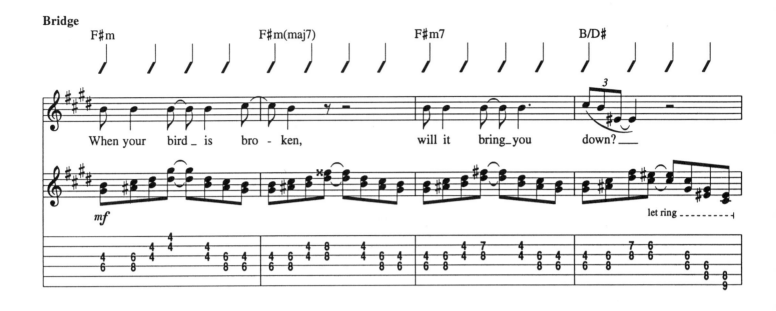

When your bird _ is bro - ken, will it bring_you down?_

You may be_ a - wo - ken, I'll be 'round,_ I'll be 'round._ You

Verse

2. tell me that you've heard ev-'ry sound _ there_ is__ and your bird can_ swing, but ya can't hear me,_

_ ya can't hear me.

Guitar Solo 2

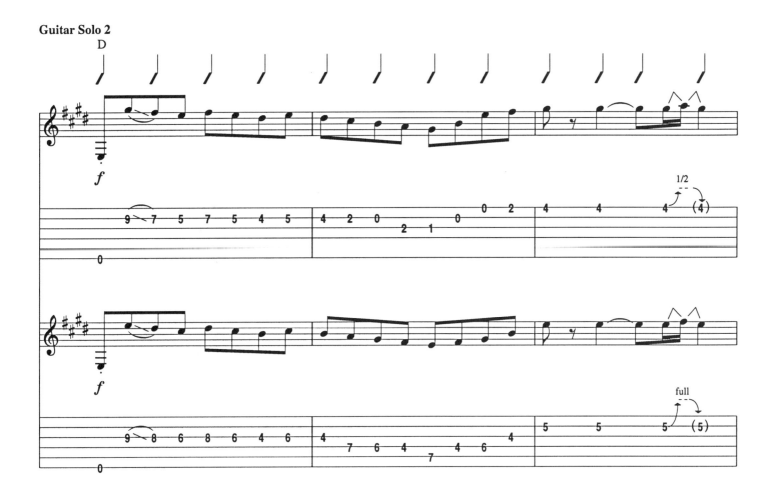

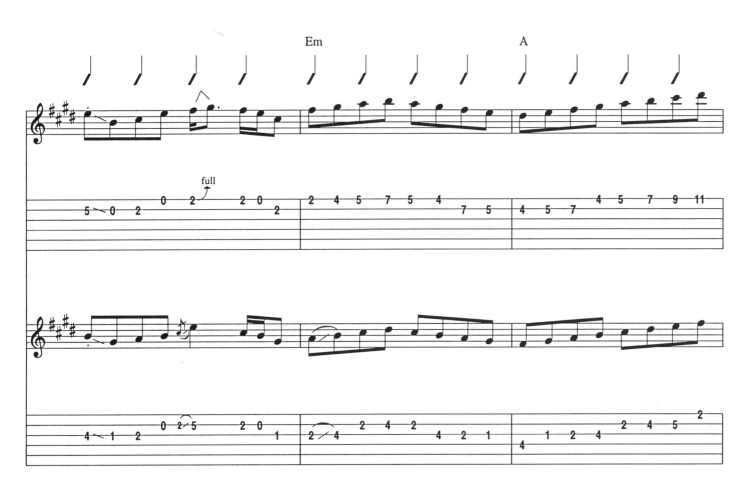

Doctor Robert

Words and Music by John Lennon and Paul McCartney

MCA music publishing

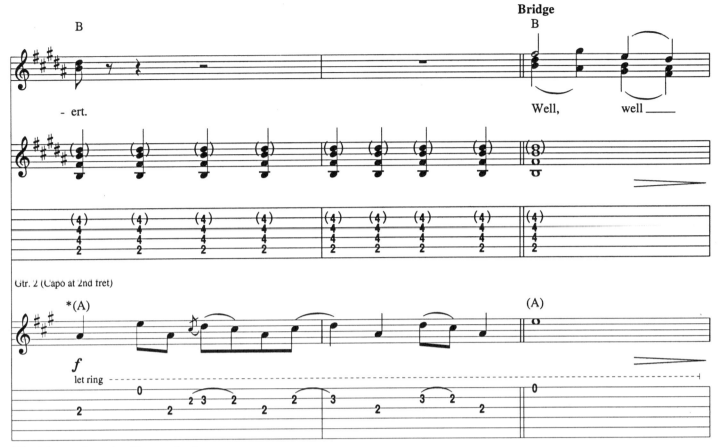

Gtr. 2 (Capo at 2nd fret)

*Chords in parentheses played by capoed guitar.

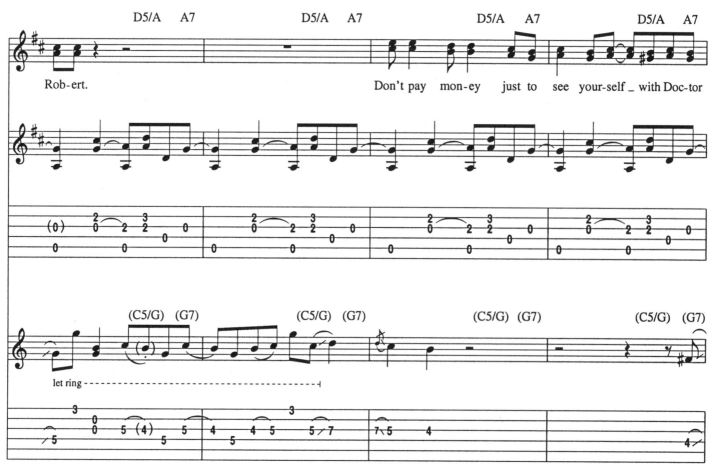

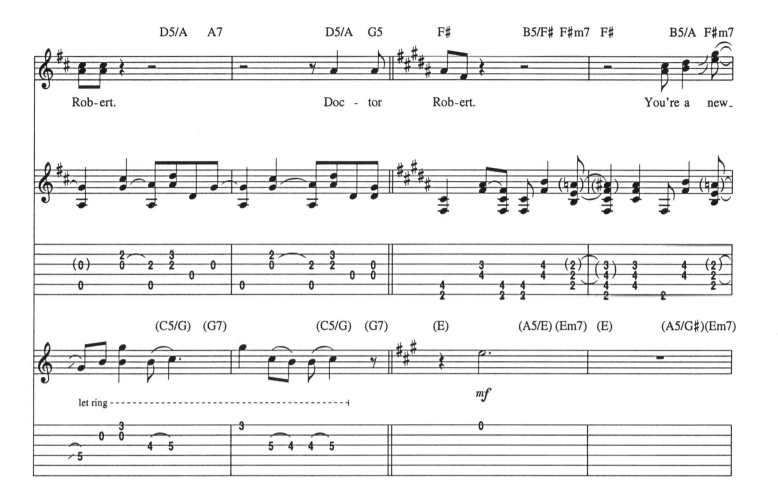

Bridge

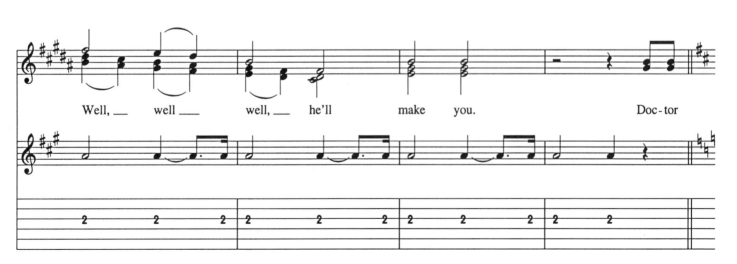

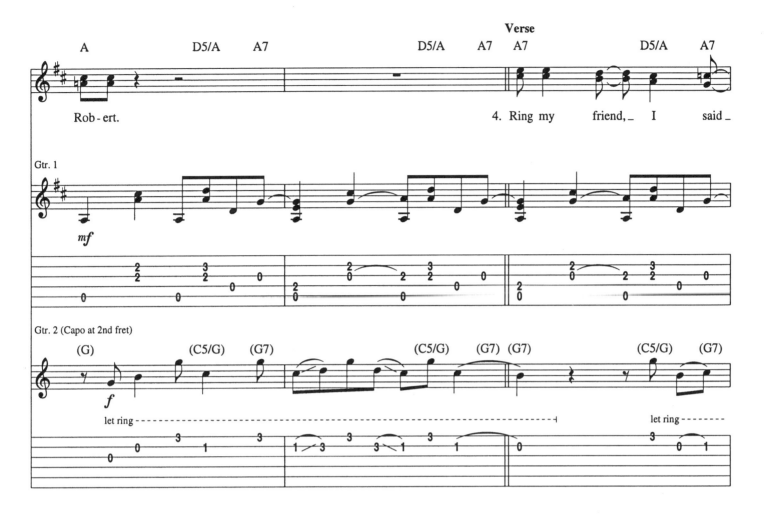

Ring my friend, I said you'd call, Doc Rob - ert. Doc-tor

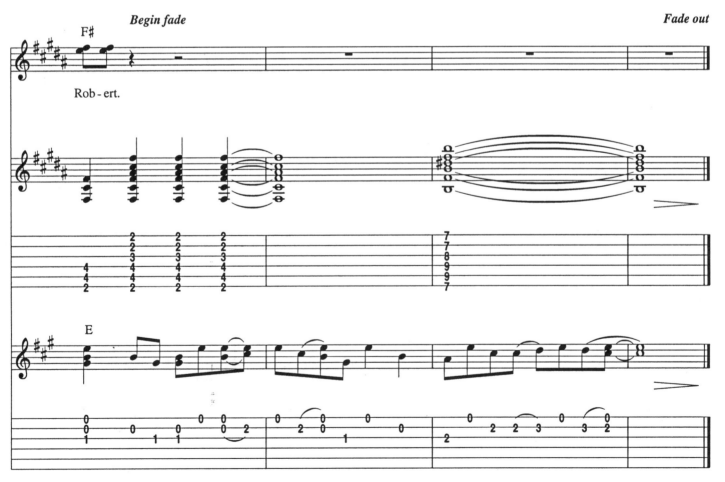

Rob - ert.

Eleanor Rigby

Words and Music by John Lennon and Paul McCartney

*w/pitch transposer (P.T.)
pre-set 8vb.
Switch on where indicated

MCA music publishing

Verse

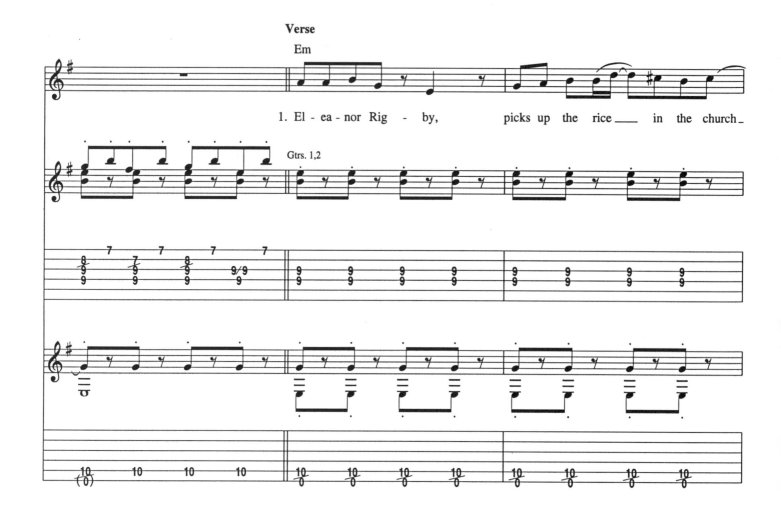

1. El - ea - nor Rig - by,   picks up the rice ___ in the church ___

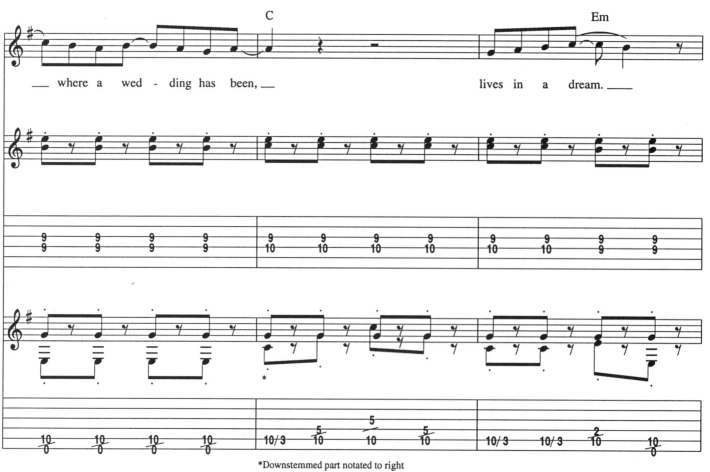

___ where a wed - ding has been, ___   lives in a dream. ___

*Downstemmed part notated to right
of / in TAB when necessary.

18

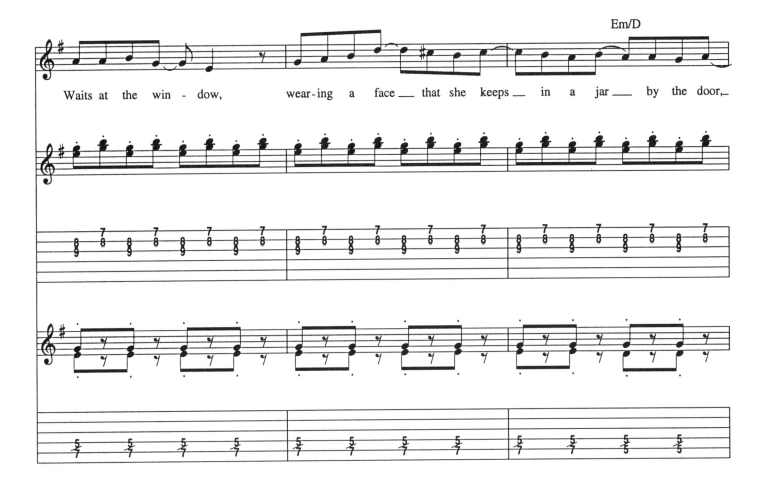

Waits at the win - dow,   wear-ing a face __ that she keeps __ in a jar __ by the door,__

Chorus 2

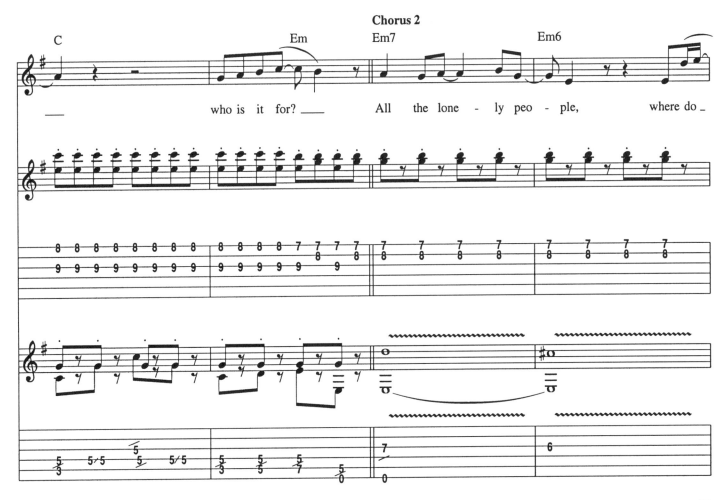

__   who is it for? __   All the lone - ly peo - ple,   where do __

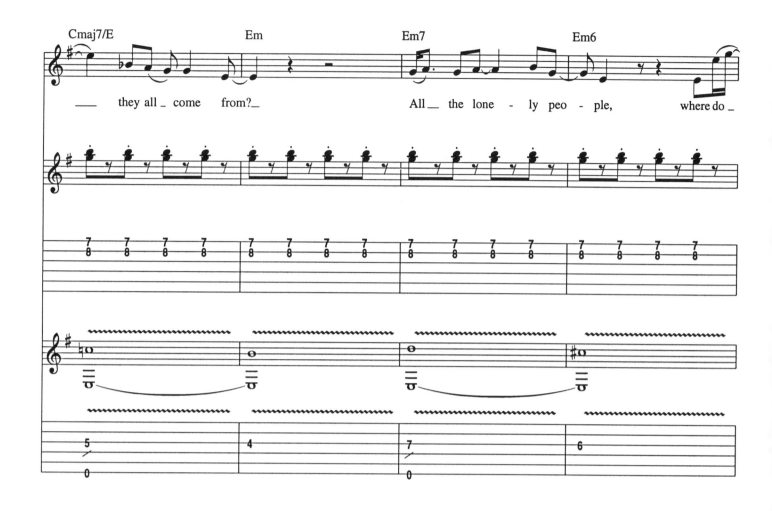

they all _ come from?_   All _ the lone - ly peo - ple,   where do _

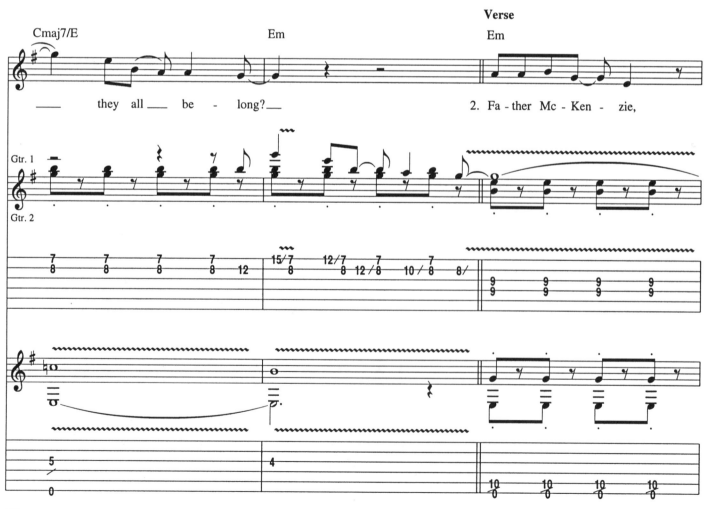

they all _ be - long?_   2. Fa - ther Mc - Ken - zie,

writ-ing the words _ of a ser - mon that no _ one will hear, _ no _

_ one comes near. _ Look at him work - ing, darn-ing his socks _ in the night _

when there's no - bod - y there. _____ What does he care? _____

Chorus 2

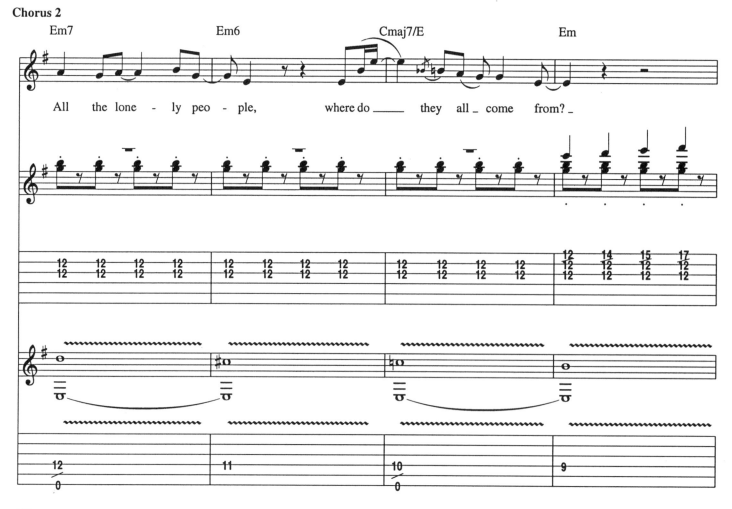

All the lone - ly peo - ple, where do _____ they all _ come from? _

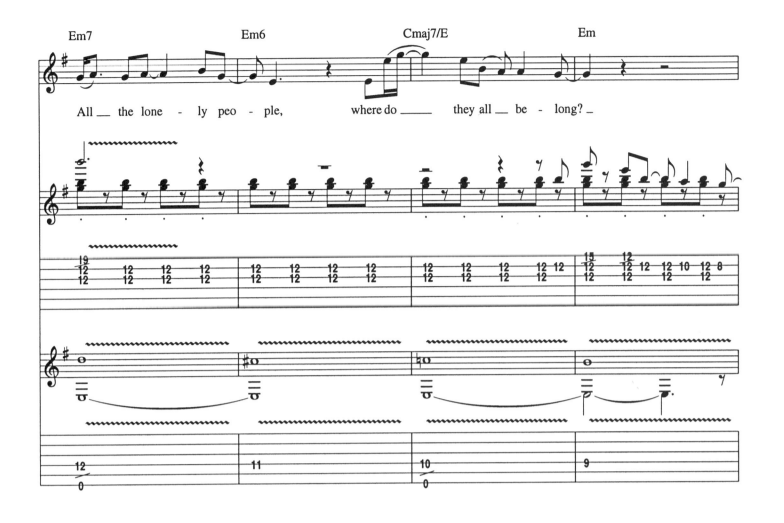

All — the lone - ly peo - ple, where do ——— they all — be - long? —

Chorus 1

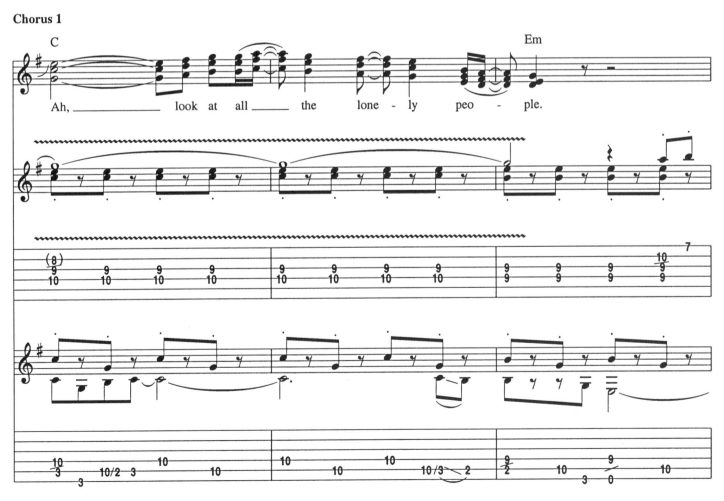

Ah, ——————— look at all ——— the lone - ly peo - ple.

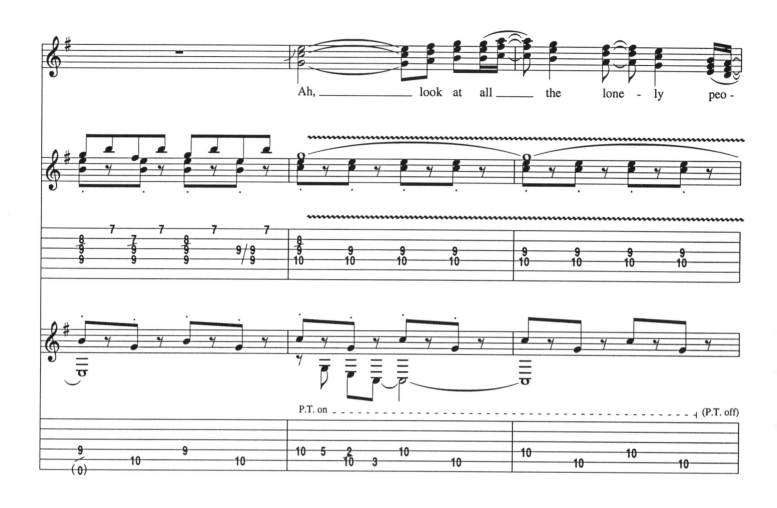

Ah, _____ look at all _____ the lone-ly peo-

3rd Verse

-ple.

3. El-ea-nor Rig - by,

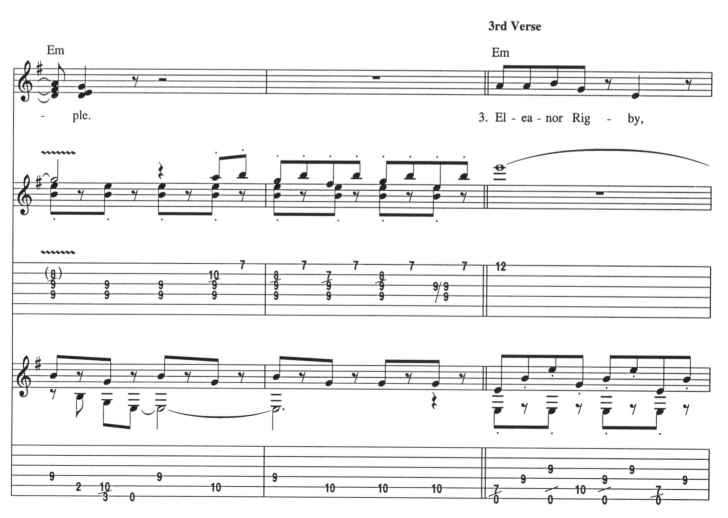

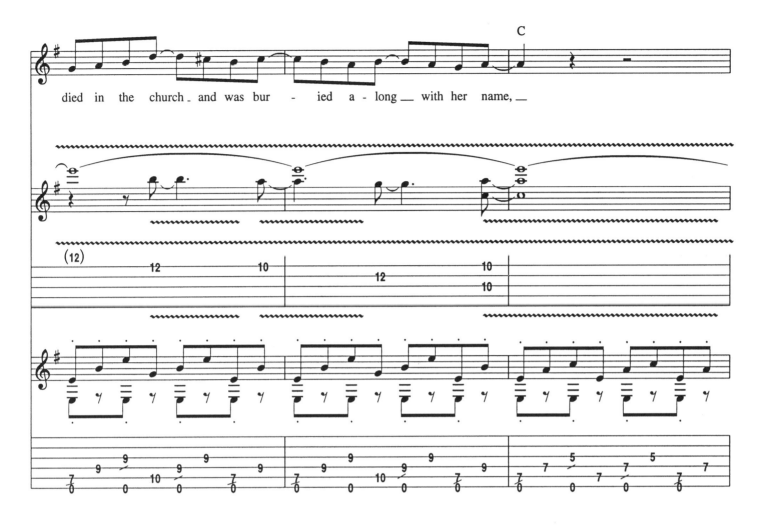

died in the church _ and was bur - ied a - long _ with her name, _

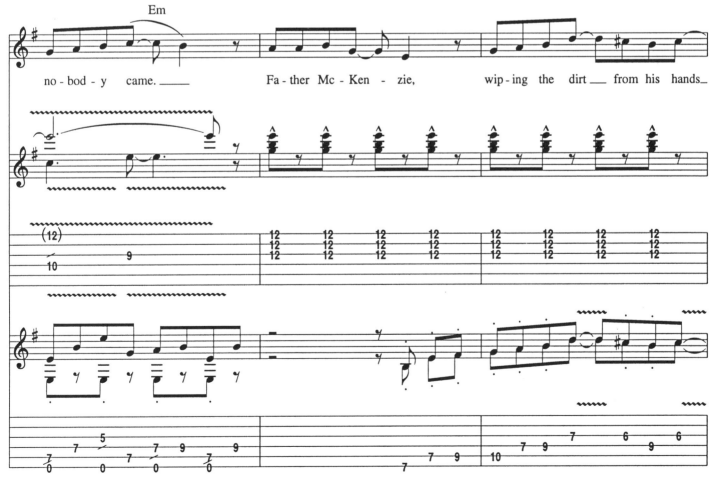

no - bod - y came. ___ Fa - ther Mc - Ken - zie, wip - ing the dirt _ from his hands _

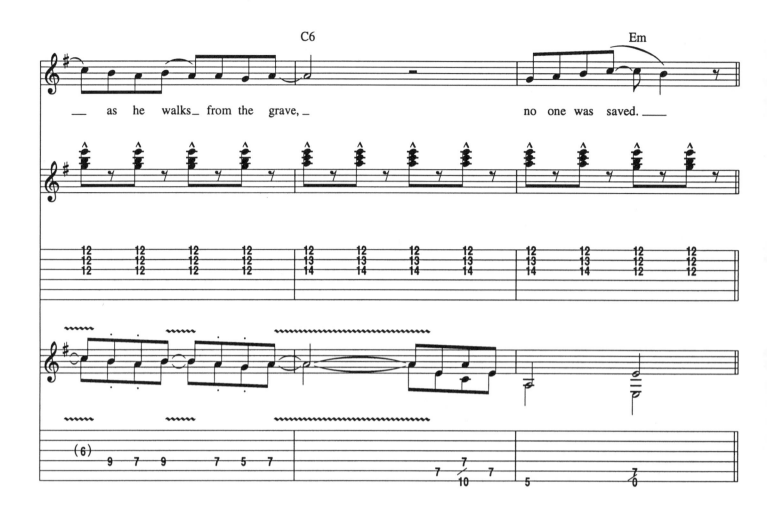

as he walks_ from the grave,_ no one was saved. ___

Chorus 2

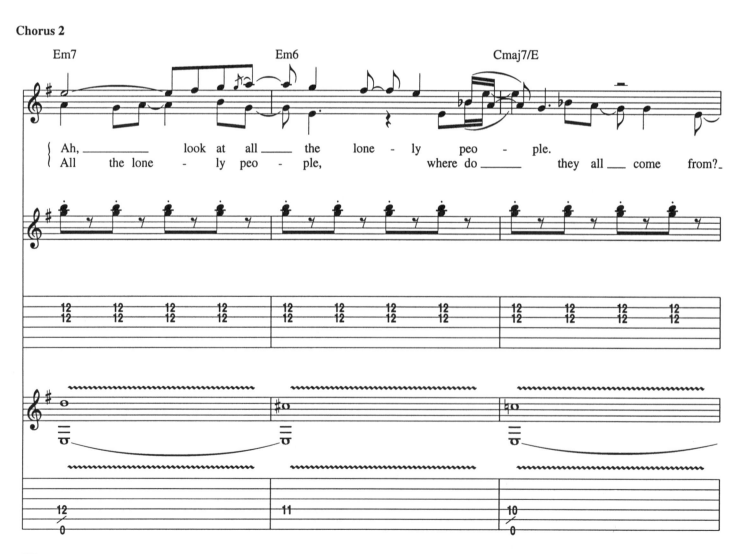

Ah, _____ look at all _____ the lone - ly peo - ple.
All the lone - ly peo - ple, where do _____ they all _____ come from?_

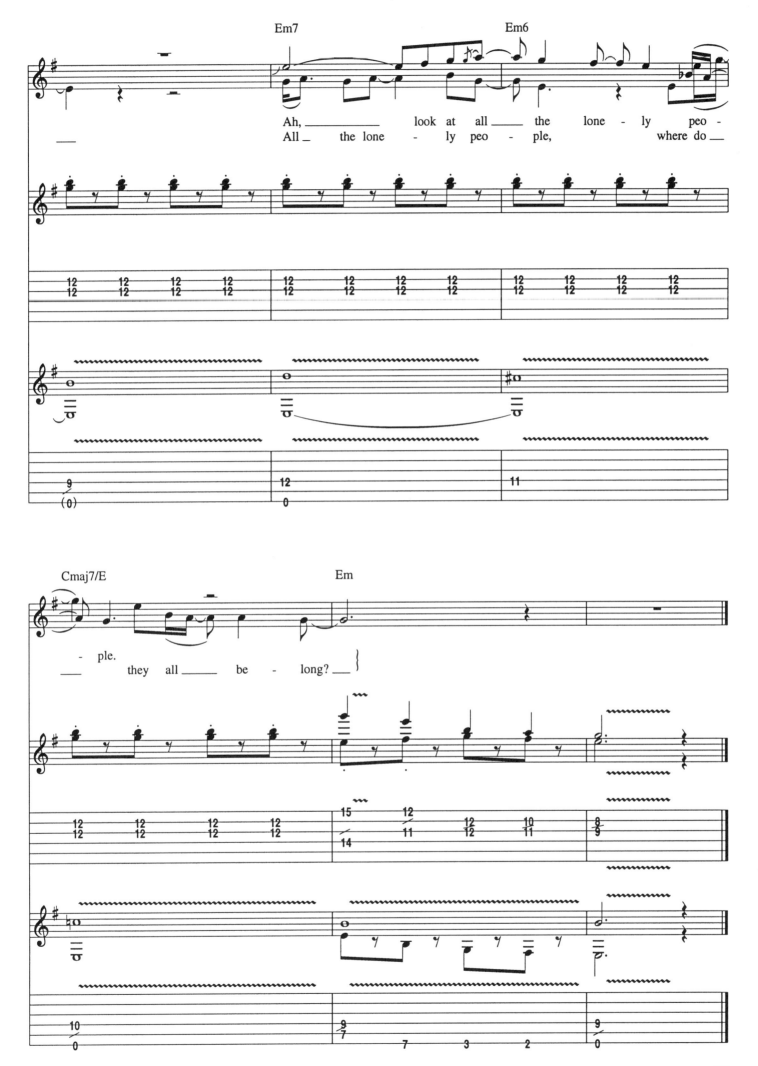

For No One

Words and Music by John Lennon and Paul McCartney

Tune Down 1/2 Step

⑥ = E♭   ③ = G♭

⑤ = A♭   ② = B♭

④ = D♭   ① = E♭

Verse

Moderately, in 2 ♩ = 160

1. Your day breaks, your mind aches, you find that all her words of kind-

Piano/Harpsichord arr. for Gtr.*

mf

*Play fingerstyle.

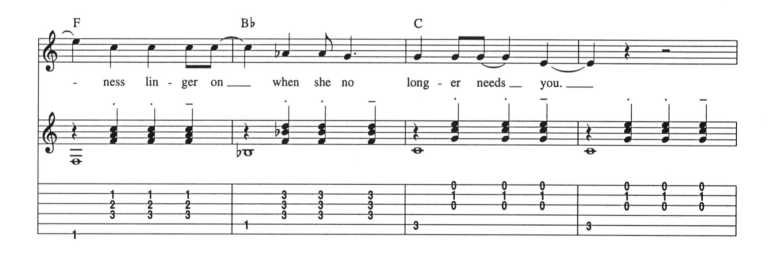

-ness linger on when she no longer needs you.

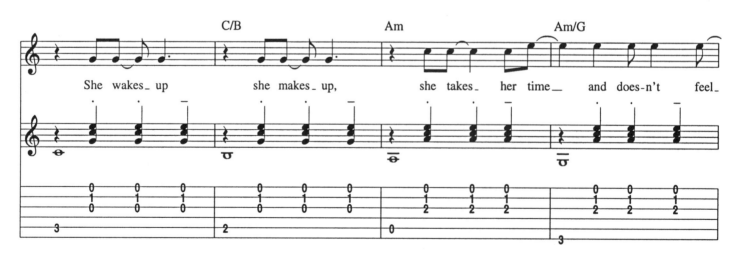

She wakes up she makes up, she takes her time and does-n't feel

MCA music publishing

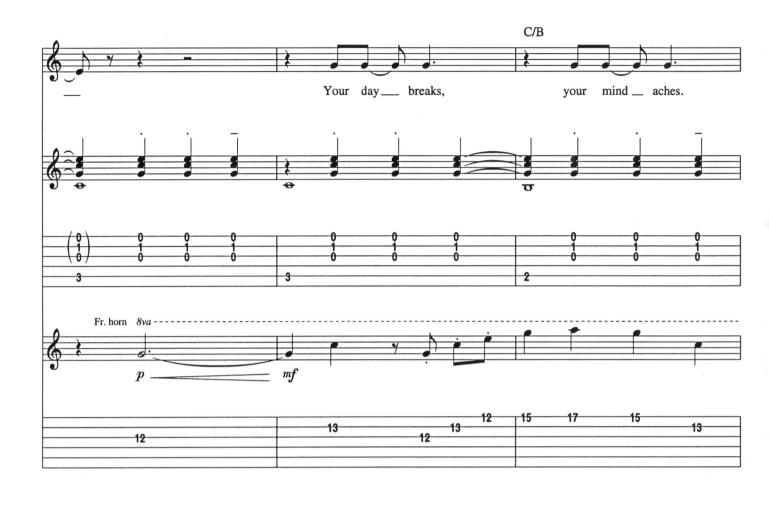

Your day___ breaks, your mind ___ aches.

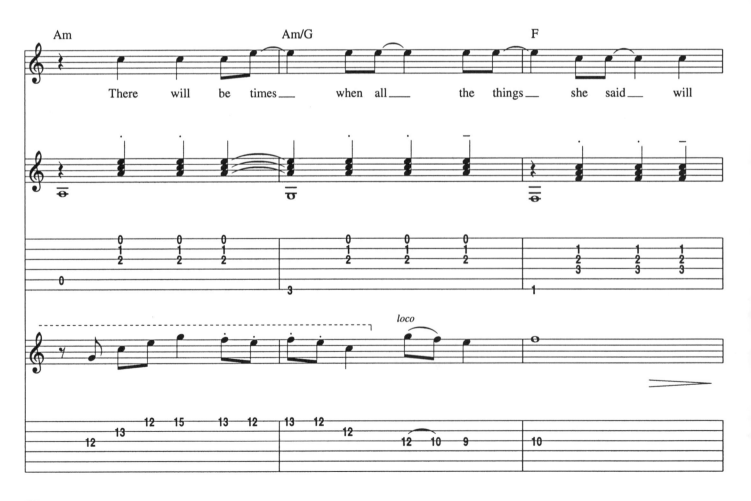

There will be times___ when all___ the things___ she said___ will

fill your head. You won't for-get her. And in her eyes

Bridge

you see noth - ing. No sign of

love be-hind the tears, cried for no - one

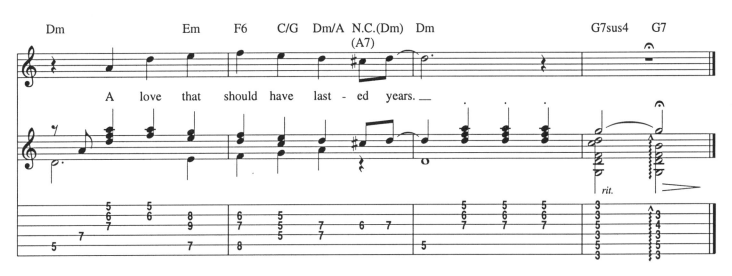

A love that should have last-ed years.

Good Day Sunshine

Words and Music by John Lennon and Paul McCartney

*Chord symbols outline overall harmony.

Good day sunshine. Good day sunshine.

Good day sunshine. 1. I need to laugh, and when the sun is out,

I've got something I can laugh about. I feel good in a special way.

*trill w/pick and middle finger.

Got To Get You Into My Life

Words and Music by John Lennon and Paul McCartney

*Gtrs. barely audible throughout verse and chorus sections.

*Bass notes played by Bass Gtr.

MCA music publishing

*Downstemmed part notated to
right of / in TAB when necessary

⊕ *Coda*

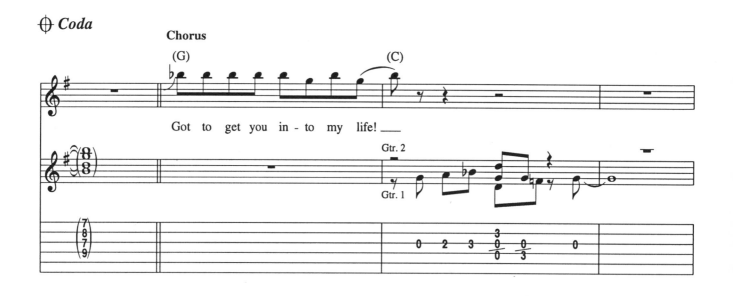

Chorus

Got to get you in-to my life! ___

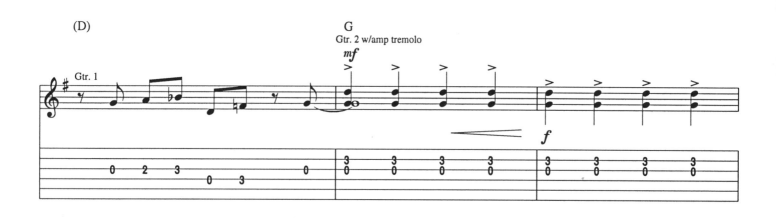

I got to get you in-to my life! ___

4. I was a-lone, _ I took a ride, I did-n't know _

_ what I would find _ there. An-oth-er road _ where may-be I _ could see an-oth - er kind of mind _ there. _ And sud-

- den-ly _ I see _ you. Did I tell _ you I need _ you _ ev'ry sin-gle day? ____

Here, There And Everywhere

Words and Music by John Lennon and Paul McCartney

nev - er - care.   But to love _ her __ is to need _ her   { 3. ev - 'ry - where, _

Ooh _____

know-ing that love _ is to share, __   each one be-liev - ing that love _ nev -er dies, __

_____ ooh, _____   ooh, _____

I Want To Tell You

Words and Music by George Harrison

MCA music publishing

I'm Only Sleeping

Words and Music by John Lennon and Paul McCartney

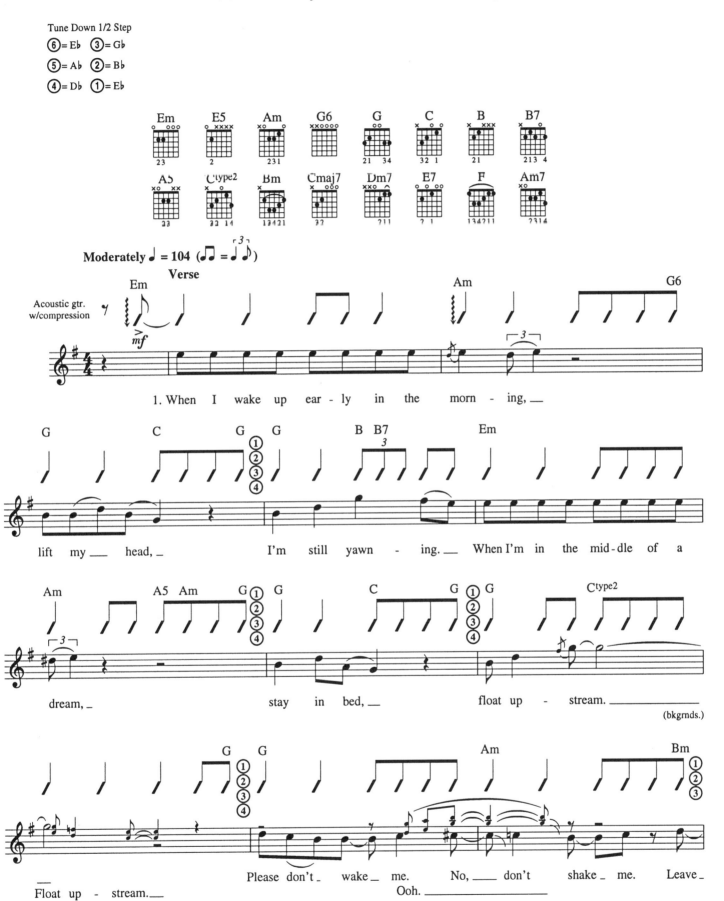

MCA music publishing

Please don't spoil __ my day. __ I'm miles __ a - way, __
(bkgrnds.) Ooh. _____

Elec. gtr. 1 tacet

Elec. gtr. 2 tacet

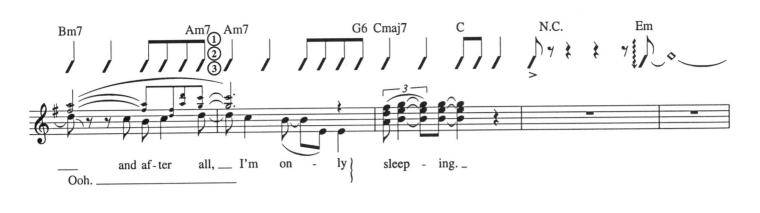

and af-ter all, __ I'm on - ly { sleep - ing. __
Ooh. _____

Bridge

Keep-in' an eye __ on the world __ go - ing by __ my __ win - dow, __ tak-in' my time. __ When __

4th Verse

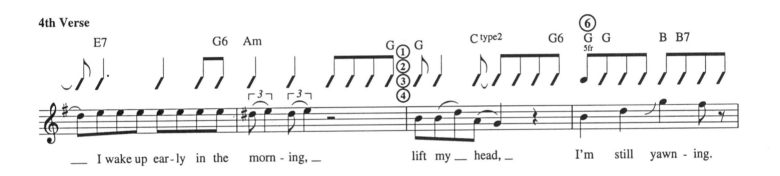

__ I wake up ear-ly in the morn - ing, __ lift my __ head, __ I'm still yawn - ing.

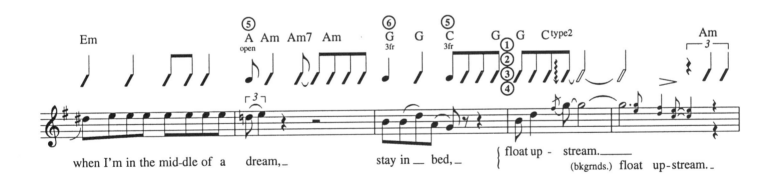

when I'm in the mid-dle of a dream, __ stay in __ bed, __ { float up - stream. ____
(bkgrnds.) float up-stream. __

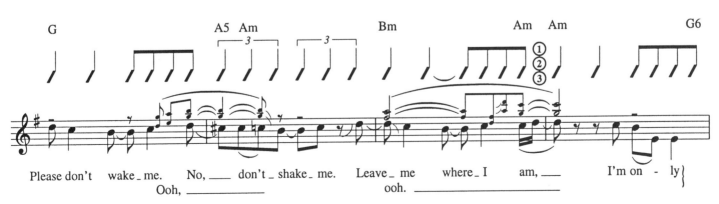

Please don't wake __ me. No, ___ don't __ shake __ me. Leave __ me where __ I am, ___ I'm on - ly {
Ooh, _____ ooh. __

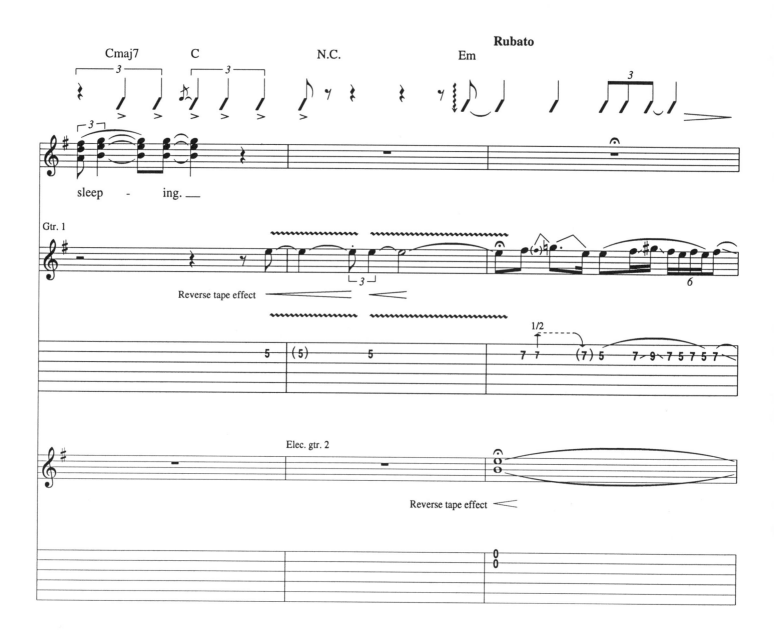

sleep - ing. ___

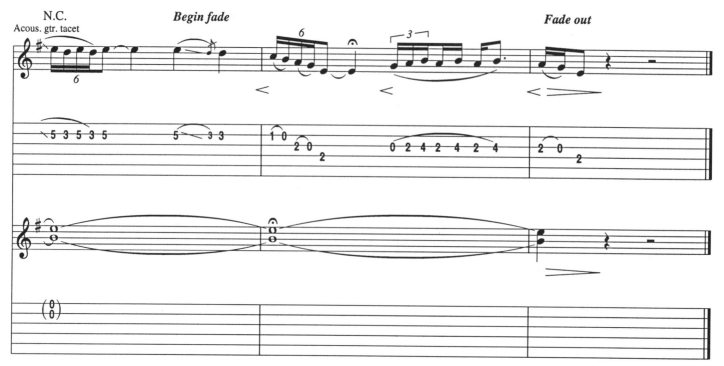

Love You To

Words and Music by George Harrison

Sitar arr. for gtr.

* ⑥ = C, ① = G

Intro

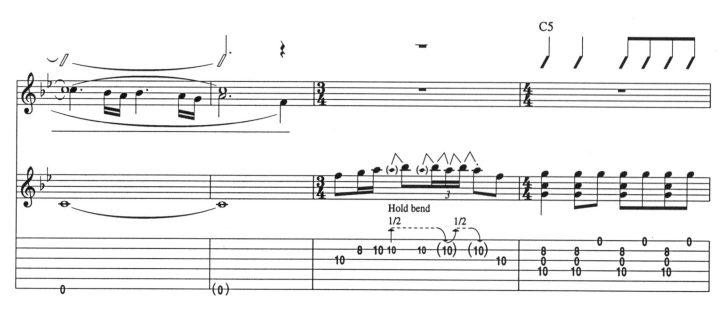

Love me while __ you can, _____ 'fore I'm a dead old man. _____

Hold bend

Hold bend

Hold even bend

** w/volume pedal and distortion

** Simulated reverse tape effect.
Swell as indicated from full off position,
then cut off sharply at grace note.

_____ 2. A __ life-

Hold bend

Elec. gtr. tacet

Verse

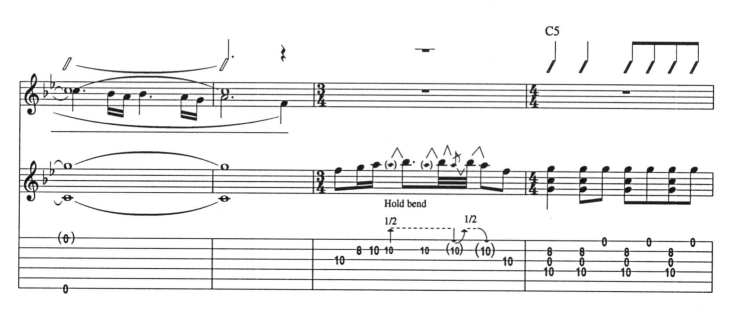

Make love all __ day long. ____ Make love sing-ing songs.__

Sitar Solo

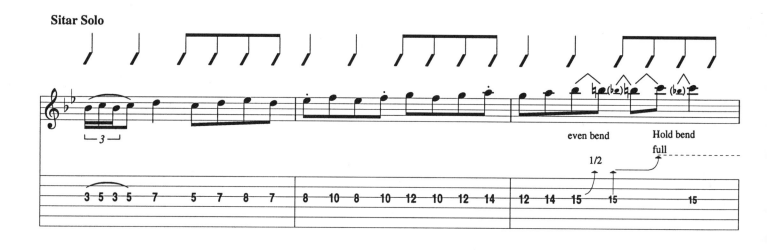

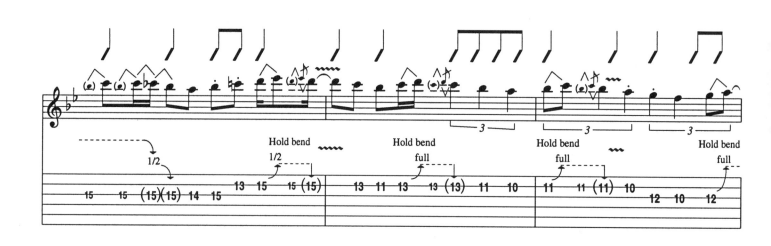

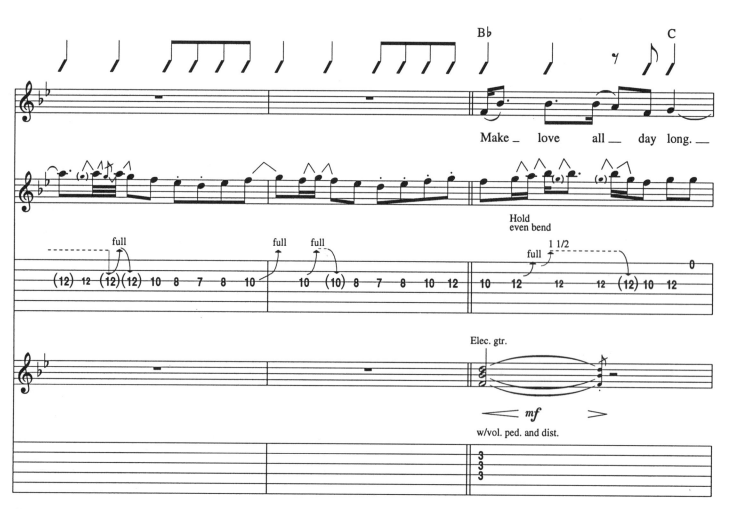

Make _ love all _ day long. _

Make love sing-ing songs. _____

Hold bend

Hold bend

Hold bend

Verse

There's peo - ple stand - ing 'round _

Hold bend

let ring

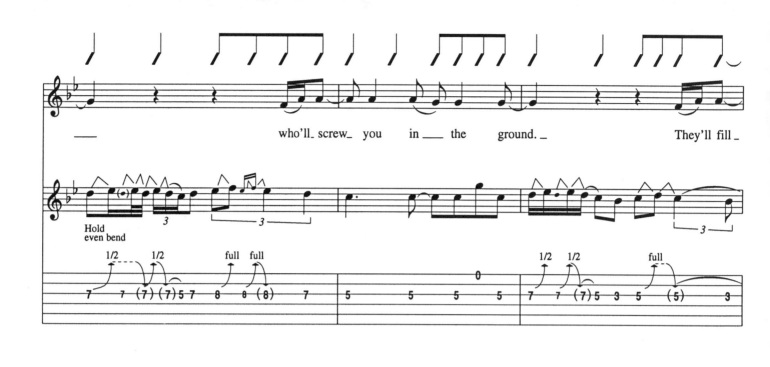

who'll screw you in the ground. They'll fill

you in with all their sins, you'll see.

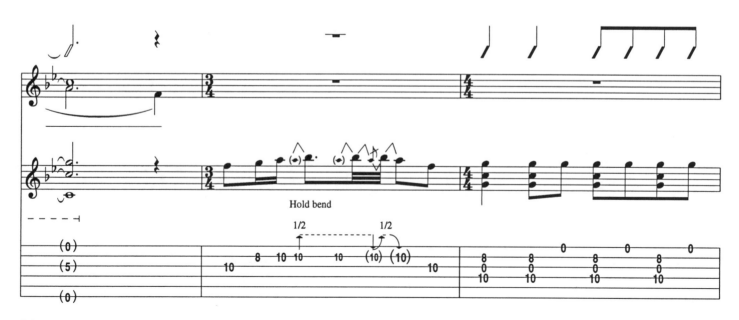

I'll make love to you _____ if you want _____ me to. _____

Sitar Solo
Faster ♩ = 150

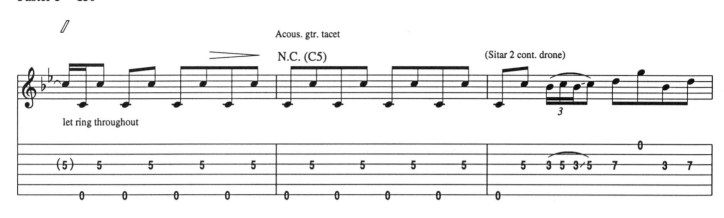

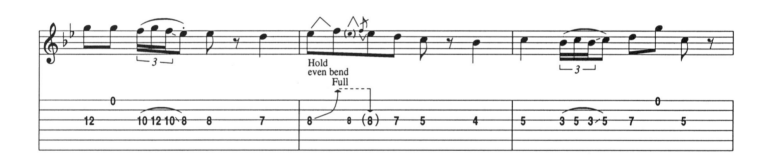

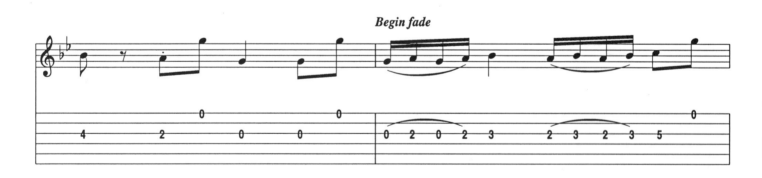

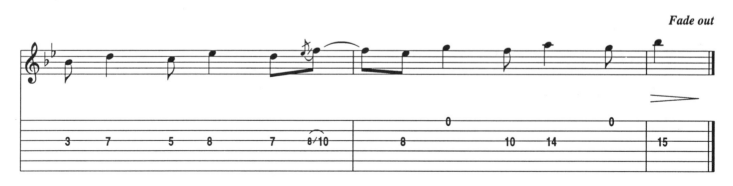

66

She Said She Said

Words and Music by John Lennon and Paul McCartney

Intro

Moderately ♩ = 108

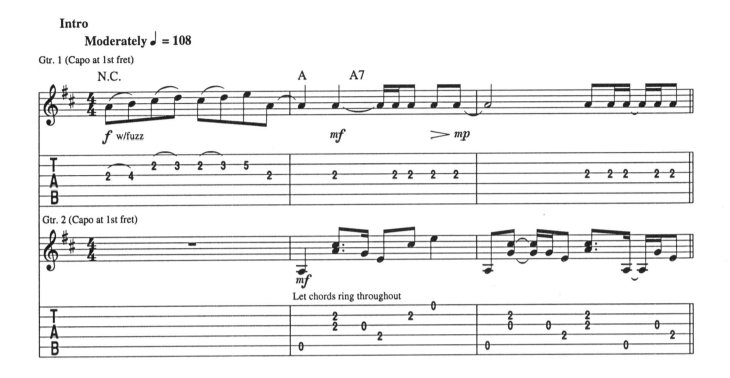

Verse

1. She said, _____ "I know what it's like to be dead, ____ I know what it

* Chords in parentheses played by capoed guitars.

** Bb bass played by bass gtr.

MCA music publishing

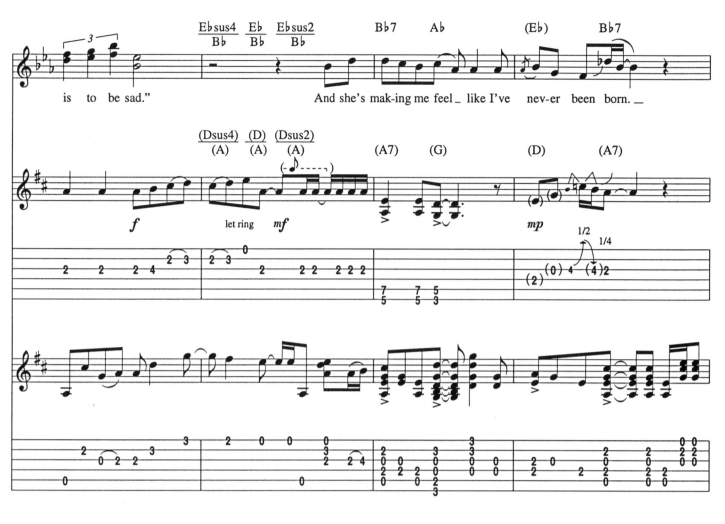

is to be sad."   And she's mak-ing me feel _ like I've nev-er been born. _

Verse

2. I   said,   "Who put all those

things in your head, ___   things that make me feel that I'm mad?   And you're

mak-ing me feel _ like I've nev-er been born."

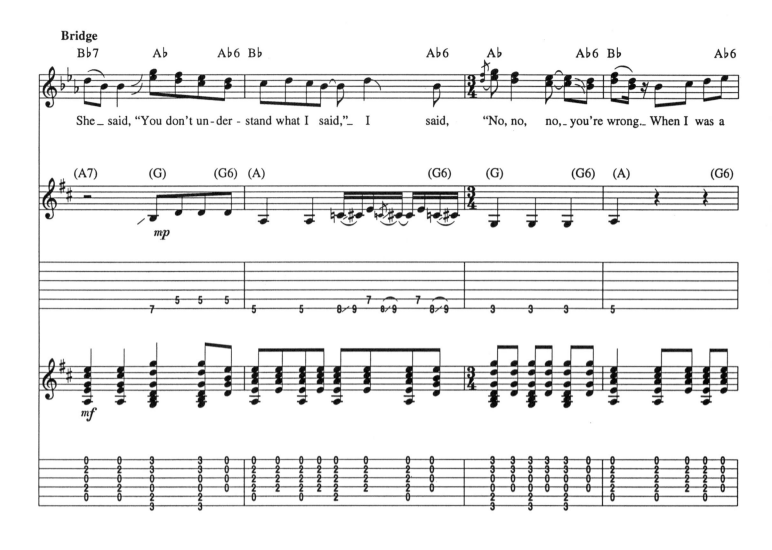

Bridge

She_ said, "You don't un-der-stand what I said,"_ I said, "No, no, no,_ you're wrong._ When I was a

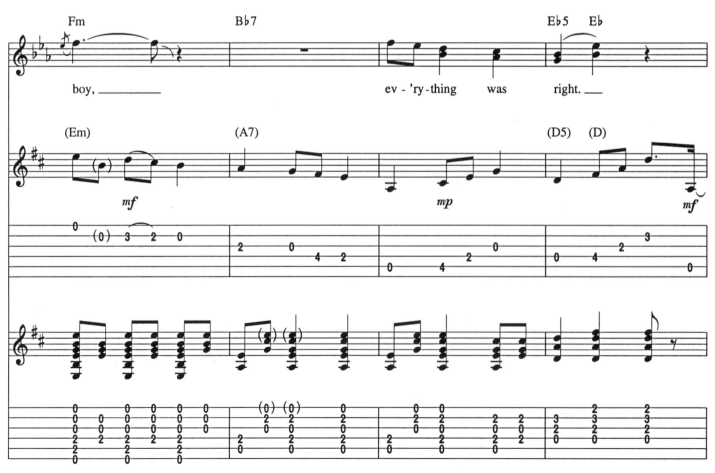

boy, _____ ev-'ry-thing was right. ___

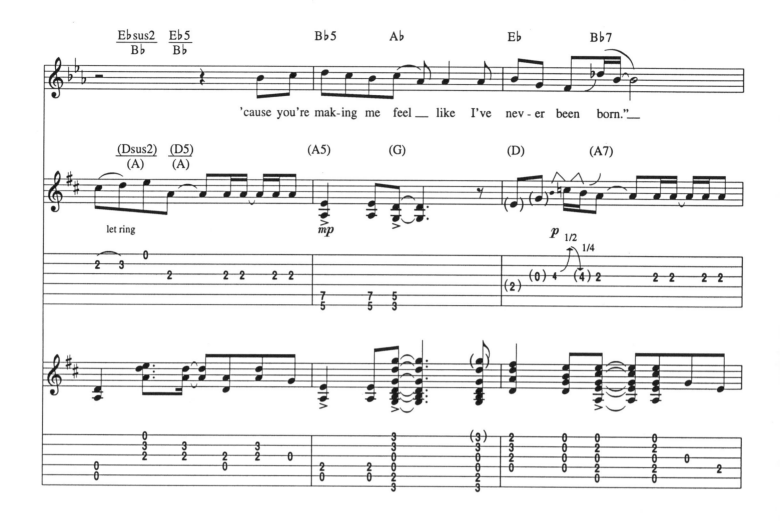

'cause you're mak-ing me feel __ like I've nev-er been born." __

let ring

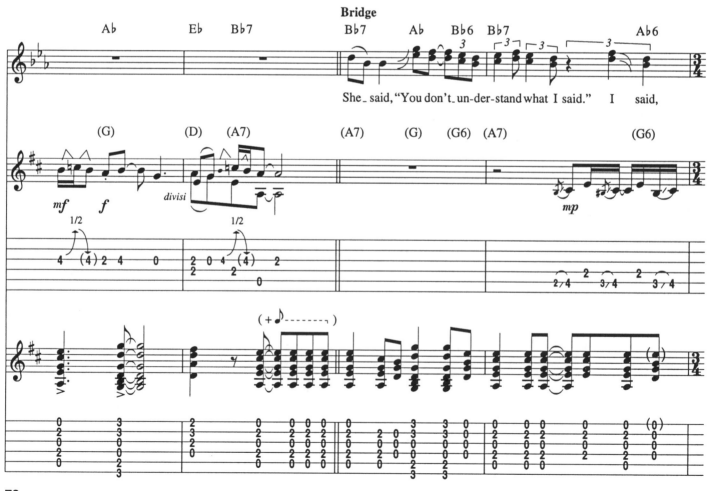

Bridge

She __ said, "You don't __ un-der-stand what I said." I said,

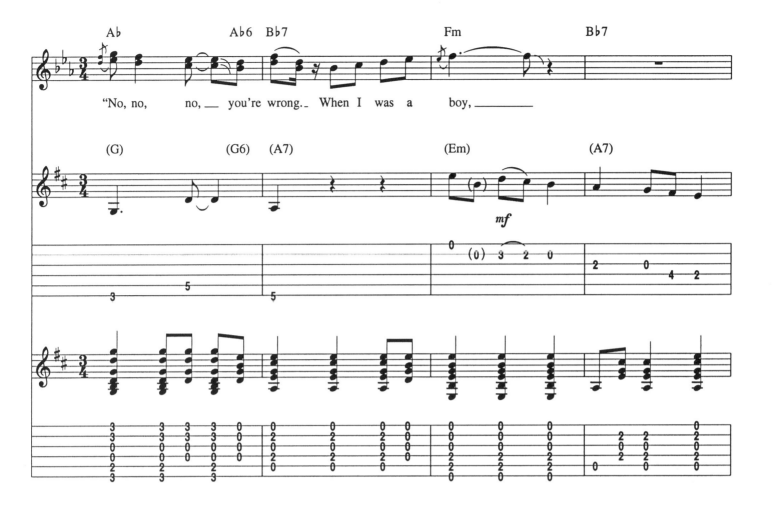

"No, no, no, — you're wrong. When I was a boy, ———

ev - 'ry - thing was right. —— Ev - 'ry - thing was

let ring - - - - - - - - - - - -

Verse

right."   4. I said, _____ "Ev-en though you know what _ you know,

I know that I'm read-y to leave,   'cause you're mak-ing me feel _ like I've

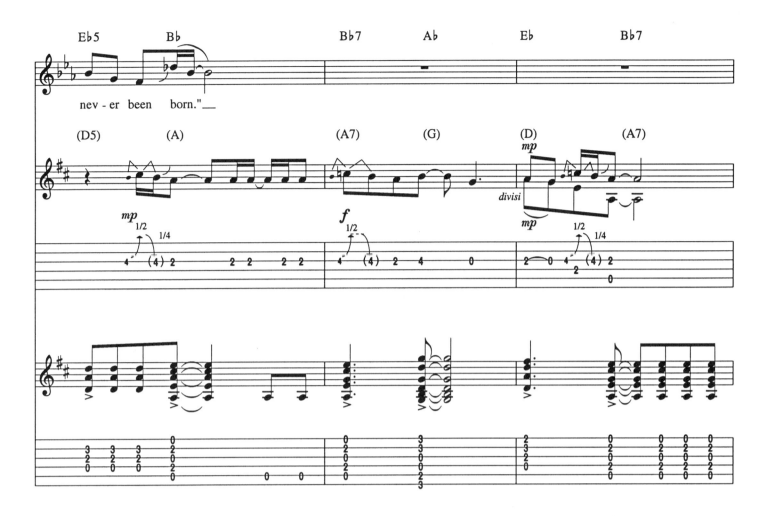

Outro

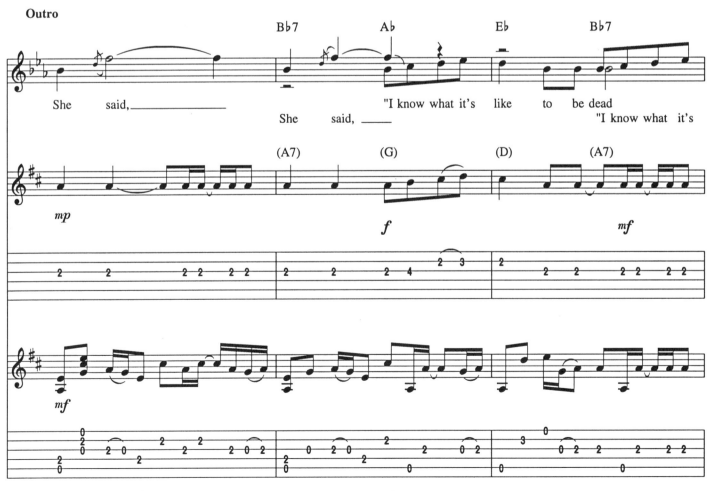

She said,_____ She said, _____ "I know what it's like to be dead

"I know what it's

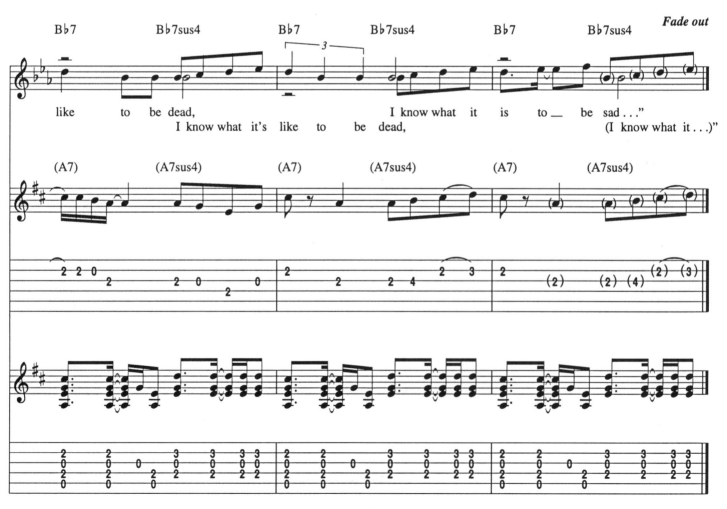

Taxman

Words and Music by George Harrison

Intro

Moderately ♩ = 138

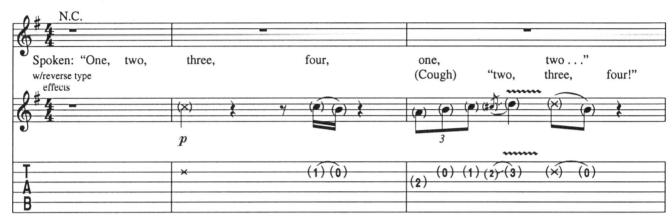

Spoken: "One, two, three, four, one, two..."
(Cough) "two, three, four!"

w/reverse type effects

Verse

1. Let me ___ tell you ___ how it ___

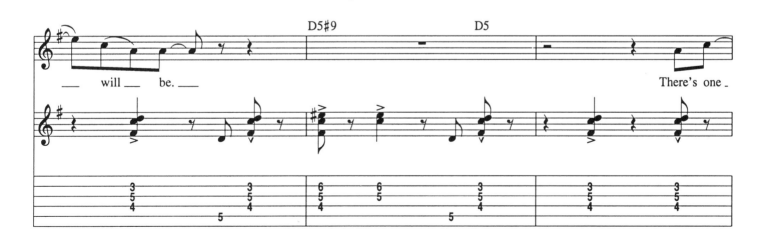

___ will ___ be. ___

There's one ___

MCA music publishing

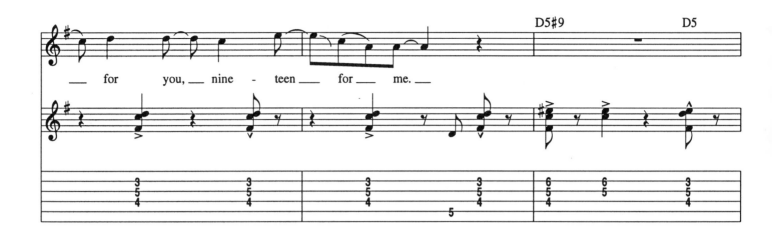

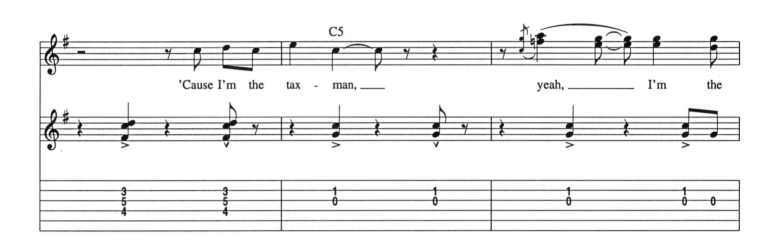

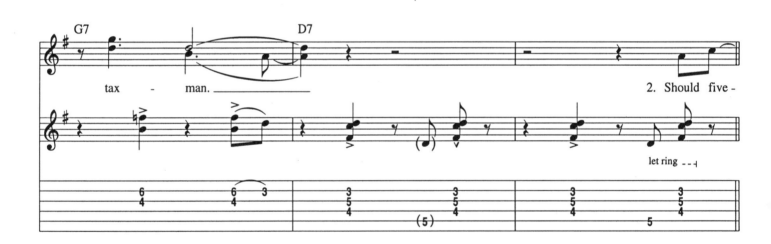

Verse

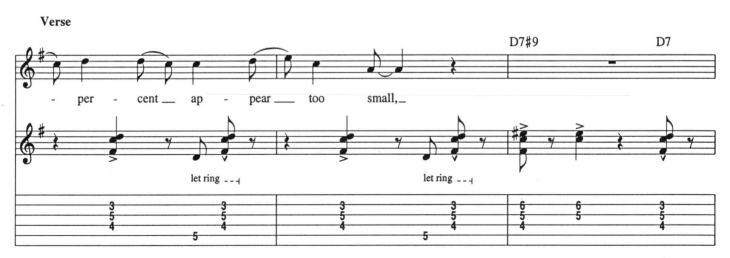

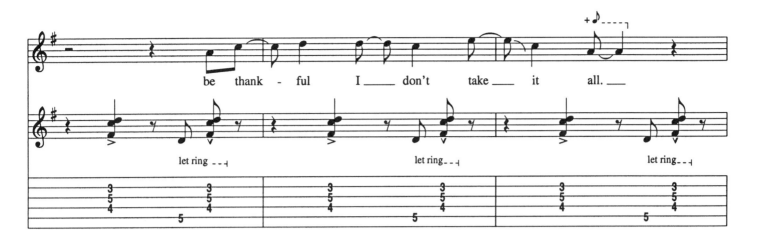

be thank-ful I ____ don't take ____ it all. ____

let ring ⌐ ¬   let ring⌐¬   let ring⌐¬

D7#9   D7   C5

'Cause I'm the tax-man,

let ring ⌐ ¬   let ring ⌐ ¬

G7   D7

yeah, _____ I'm the tax - man. _____

Bridge

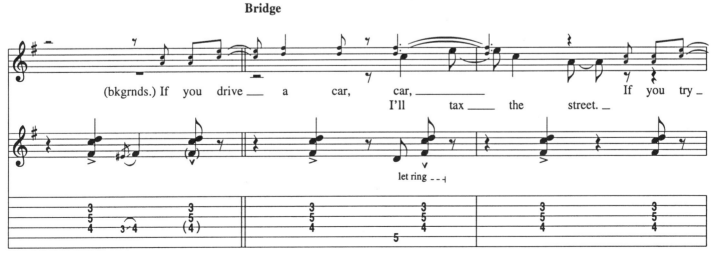

(bkgrnds.) If you drive ____ a car, car, _____   If you try ____
I'll tax ____ the street. ____

let ring ⌐ ¬

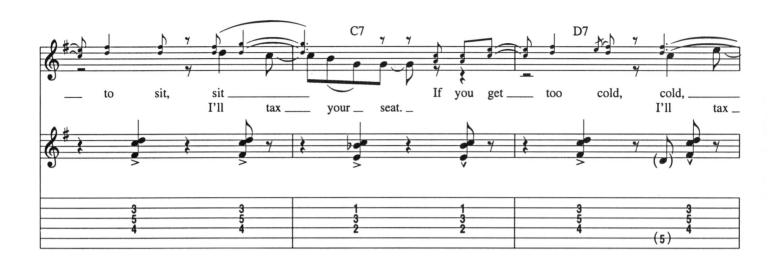

— to sit, sit _____
I'll tax ___ your ___ seat. ___
If you get ___ too cold, cold, _____
I'll tax ___

— the heat. ___
If you take ___ a walk, walk, _____
I'll ___ tax ___ your ___ feet. ___

let ring

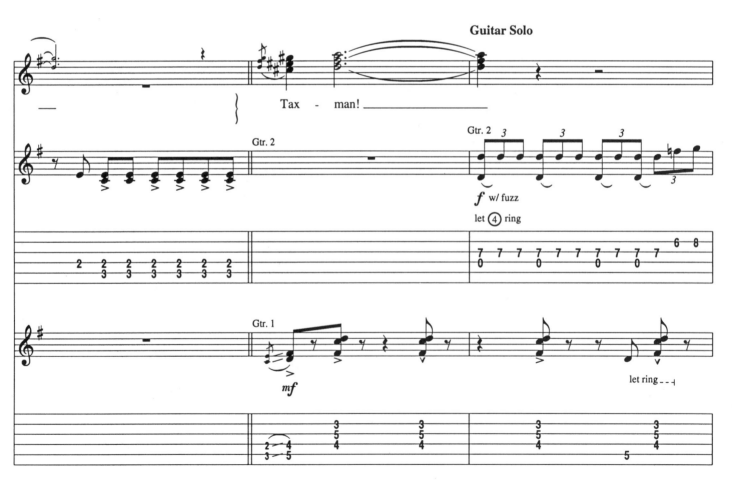

Guitar Solo

Tax - man! _____

Gtr. 2

f w/ fuzz

let ④ ring

Gtr. 2

Gtr. 1

mf

let ring

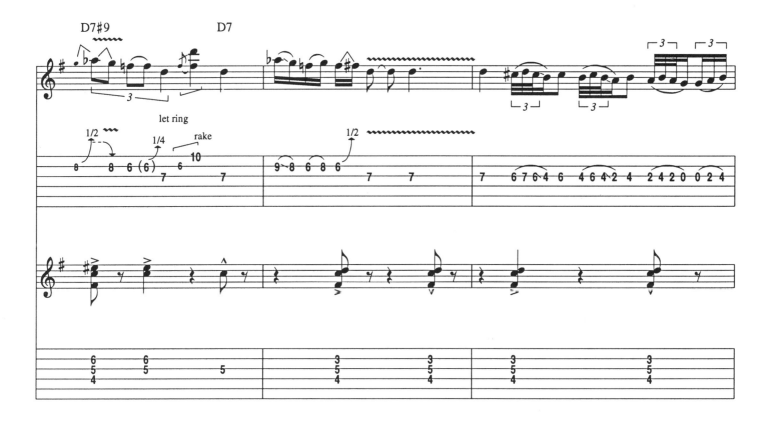

'Cause I'm   the

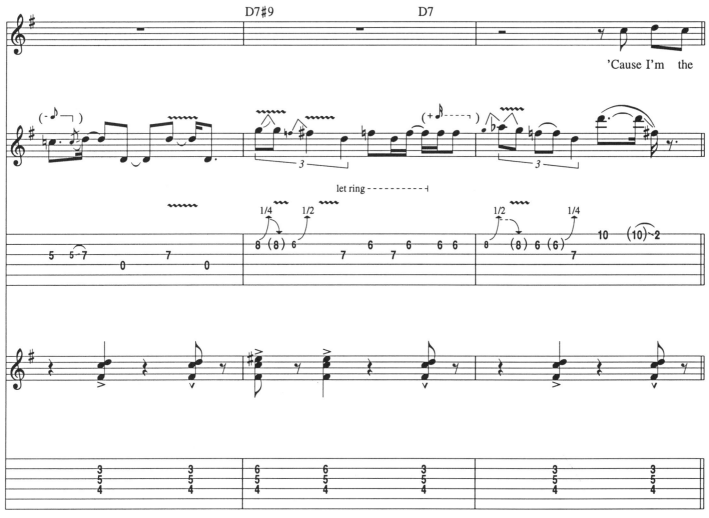

tax - man, __ yeah, __ I'm the tax - man. __

Verse

3. Don't ask __ me what __ I want __ it for. __

(bkgrnds.) Ah, ah, __ mis-ter Wil-

even bend

even bend

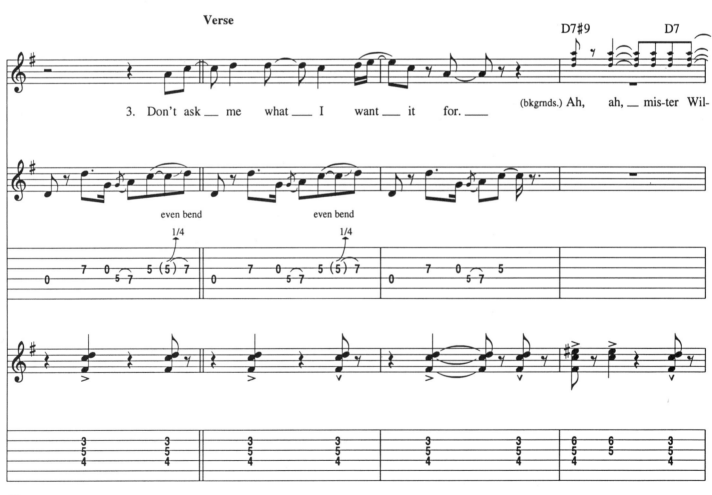

son. If you _ don't want _ to pay _ some more. _ Ah, ah, _ Mis-ter Heath..

_ 'Cause I'm the tax-man, yeah, ___ I'm the tax - man. ___

Verse

4. Now my __ ad - vice __ for those __ who die. __

let ring __

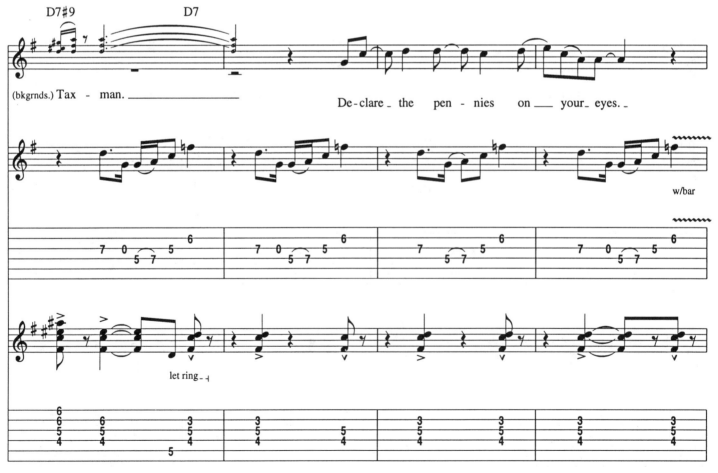

(bkgrnds.) Tax - man. _____

De - clare __ the pen - nies on __ your __ eyes. __

w/bar

let ring __

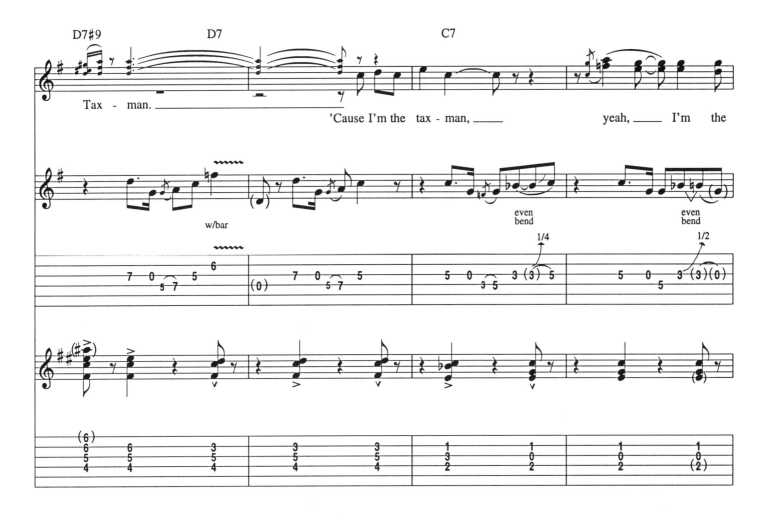

Tax - man. _____ 'Cause I'm the tax - man, _____ yeah, _____ I'm the

tax - man, _____ and you're _____ work - ing for no one but _____

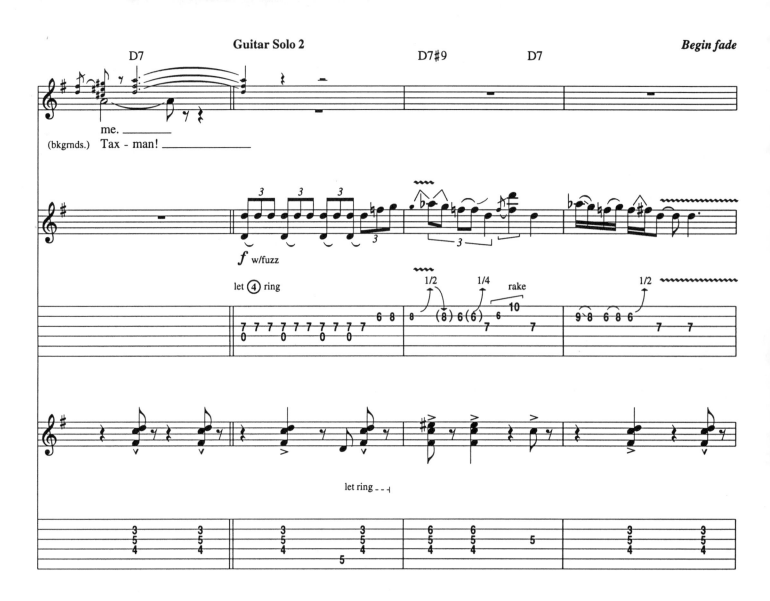

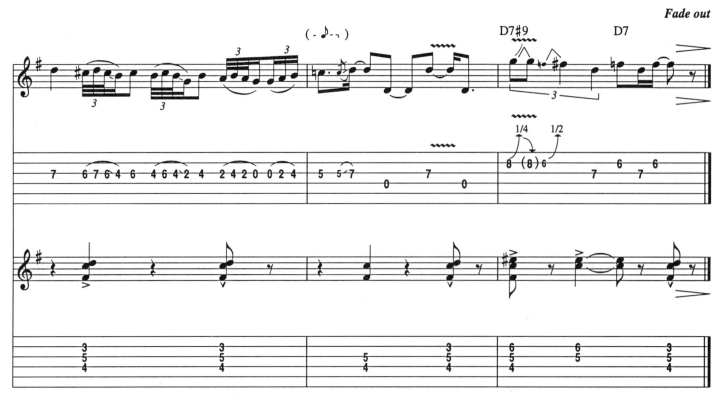

Tomorrow Never Knows

Words and Music by John Lennon and Paul McCartney

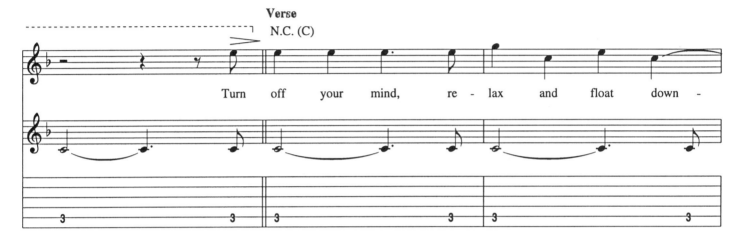

Turn off your mind, re - lax and float down -

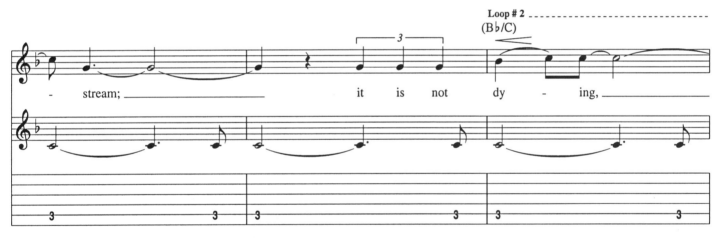

- stream; it is not dy - ing,

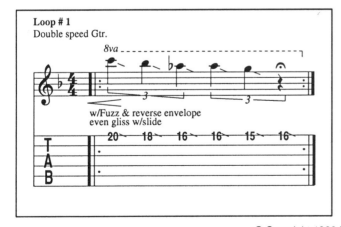

Loop # 1
Double speed Gtr.

w/Fuzz & reverse envelope
even gliss w/slide

Loop # 2
Organ arr. for Gtr.

MCA music publishing

Backwards Gtr. solo

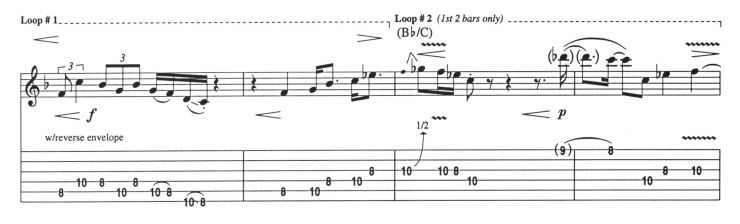

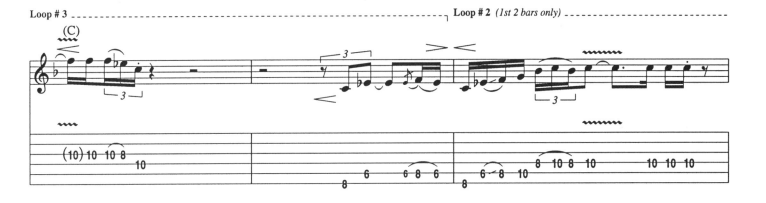

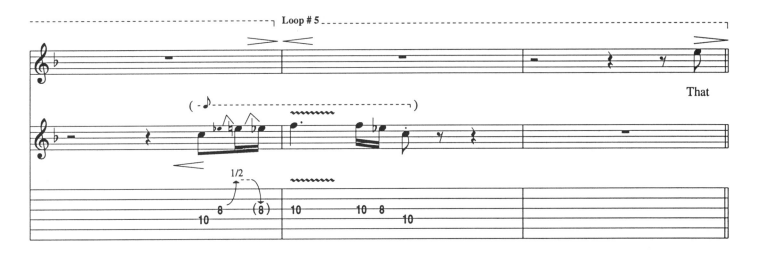

Verse

love is all, _____ that love _____ is ev - 'ry - one; _____

pitch: G

Yellow Submarine

Words and Music by John Lennon and Paul McCartney

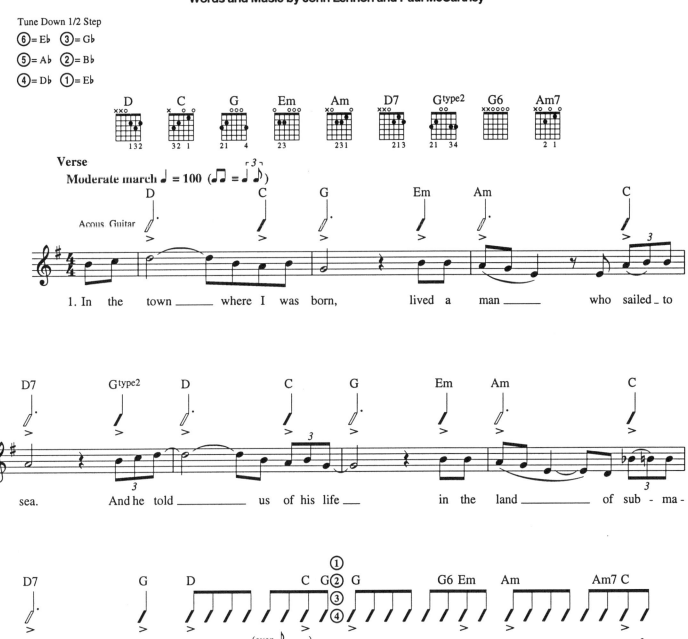

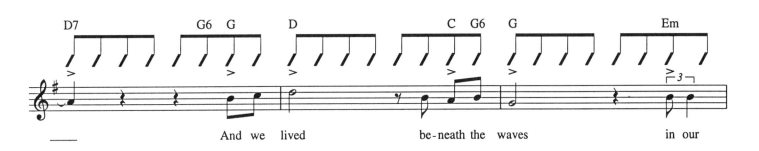

MCA music publishing

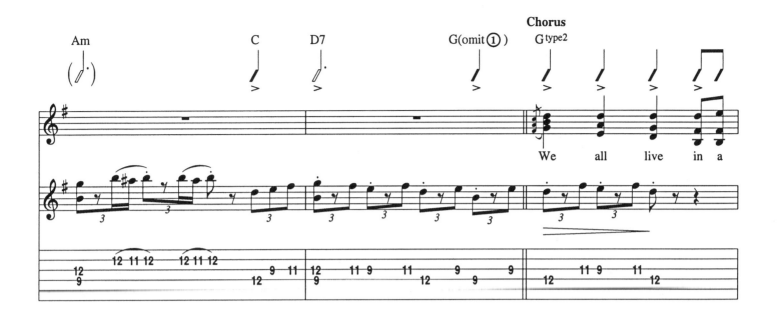

We all live in a

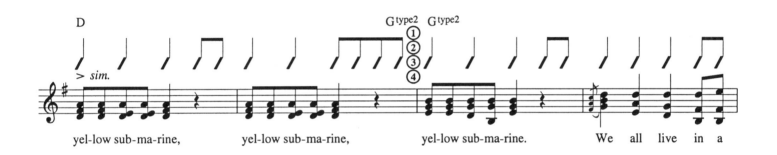

yel-low sub-ma-rine,   yel-low sub-ma-rine,   yel-low sub-ma-rine.   We all live in a

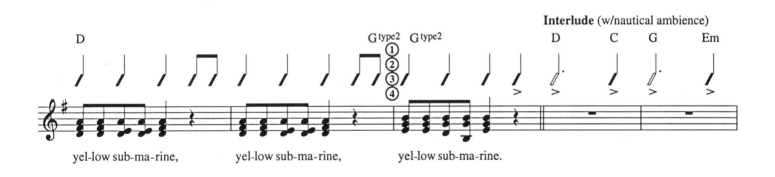

yel-low sub-ma-rine,   yel-low sub-ma-rine,   yel-low sub-ma-rine.

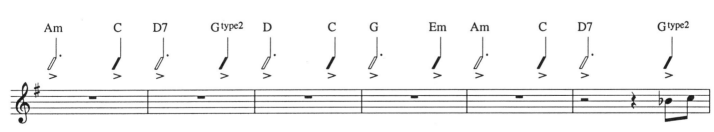

3. As we

Verse

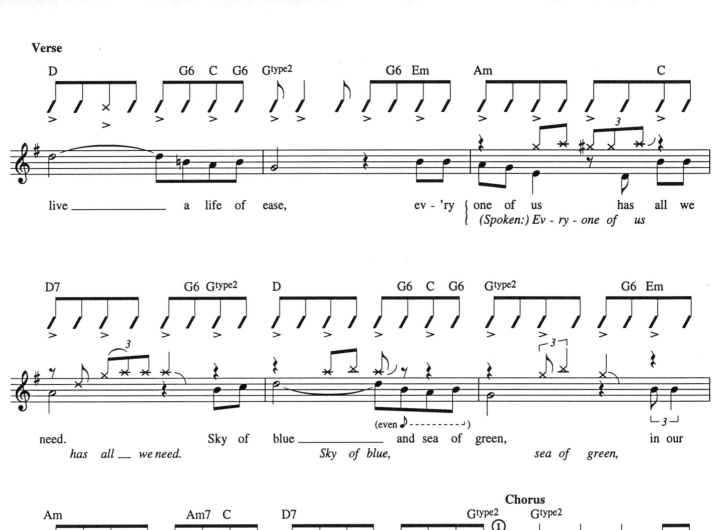

live _____ a life of ease, ev - 'ry { one of us has all we
(Spoken:) Ev - ry - one of us

need. Sky of blue _____ and sea of green, in our
has all __ we need. (even ♪----------♩) Sky of blue, sea of green,

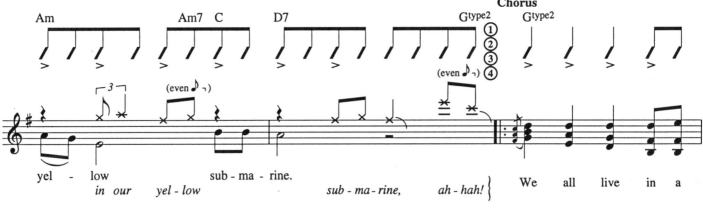

Chorus

yel - low sub - ma - rine. We all live in a
in our yel - low sub - ma - rine, ah - hah! }

yel - low sub - ma - rine, yel - low sub - ma - rine, yel - low sub - ma - rine.

Repeat and Fade

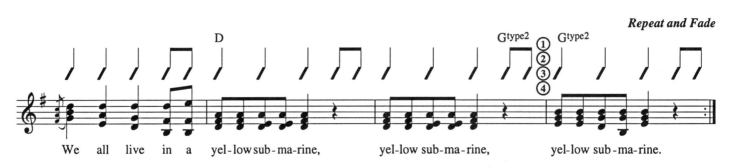

We all live in a yel-low sub-ma-rine, yel-low sub-ma-rine, yel-low sub-ma-rine.

NOTATION LEGEND

RECORDED VERSIONS

GUITAR
RECORDED VERSIONS GUITAR

The Best Note-For-Note Transcriptions Availab...

ALL BOOKS INCLUDE TABLATURE

00692015 Aerosmith's Greatest Hits.....................$18.95	00694894 Frank Gambale – The Great Explorers.....$18.95	00694868 Gary Moore – After Hours ....$18.
00660133 Aerosmith – Pump....................................$18.95	00694807 Danny Gatton – 88 Elmira St.................$17.95	00694849 Gary Moore – The Early Years ....$18.
00694865 Alice In Chains – Dirt $18.95	00694848 Genuine Rockabilly Guitar Hits $19.95	00694872 Vinnie Moore – Meltdown ....$18.
00660225 Alice In Chains – Facelift $18.95	00660326 Guitar Heroes $17.95	00694883 Nirvana – Nevermind ....$18.
00694826 Anthrax – Attack Of The Killer B's...........$18.95	00694780 Guitar School Classics..............................$17.95	00694847 Ozzy Osbourne – The Best Of Ozzy ....$22.
00660227 Anthrax – Persistence Of Time................$18.95	00694768 Guitar School Greatest Hits......................$17.95	00694830 Ozzy Osbourne – No More Tears.............$18.
00694797 Armored Saint – Symbol Of Salvation........$18.95	00694854 Buddy Guy – Damn Right,	00694855 Pearl Jam – Ten...$18.9
00660051 Badlands $18.95	I've Got The Blues...................................$18.95	00693800 Pink Floyd – Early Classics $18.9
00694863 Beatles – Sgt. Pepper's Lonely	00660325 The Harder Edge $17.95	00660188 Poison – Flesh & Blood $18.9
Hearts Club Band..$18.95	00694798 George Harrison Anthology......................$19.95	00693865 Poison – Look What The Cat Dragged In..$18.9
00694832 Beatles – Acoustic Guitar Book................$18.95	00692930 Jimi Hendrix-Are You Experienced?........$19.95	00693864 The Best Of Police $18.9
00694880 The Beatles – Abbey Road $18.95	00692931 Jimi Hendrix-Axis: Bold As Love............$19.95	00692535 Elvis Presley..$18.9
00660140 The Beatles Guitar Book $18.95	00660192 The Jimi Hendrix Concerts.......................$24.95	00693910 Ratt – Invasion of Your Privacy $18.9
00694891 The Beatles – Revolver $18.95	00692932 Jimi Hendrix-Electric Ladyland $24.95	00693911 Ratt – Out Of The Cellar...........................$18.9
00694884 The Best of George Benson $19.95	00660099 Jimi Hendrix-Radio One $24.95	00660060 Robbie Robertson $18.9
00692385 Chuck Berry $18.95	00660024 Jimi Hendrix-Variations On A Theme:	00694760 Rock Classics $17.9
00692200 Black Sabbath – We Sold Our Soul	Red House $18.95	00693474 Rock Superstars $17.9
For Rock 'N' Roll......................................$18.95	00660029 Buddy Holly $18.95	00694836 Richie Sambora – Stranger In This Town.$18.9
00694821 Blue Heaven – Great Blues Guitar $18.95	00660200 John Lee Hooker – The Healer $18.95	00694805 Scorpions – Crazy World $18.9
00694770 Jon Bon Jovi – Blaze Of Glory $18.95	00660169 John Lee Hooker – A Blues Legend............$17.95	00694885 Spin Doctors $18.9
00694871 Bon Jovi – Keep The Faith.......................$18.95	00694850 Iron Maiden – Fear Of The Dark $19.95	00694796 Steelheart $18.9
00694774 Bon Jovi – New Jersey.............................$18.95	00694761 Iron Maiden – No Prayer For The Dying ..$18.95	00694180 Stryper – In God We Trust $18.9
00694775 Bon Jovi – Slippery When Wet..................$18.95	00693096 Iron Maiden – Power Slave/	00694824 Best Of James Taylor $14.9
00694762 Cinderella – Heartbreak Station $18.95	Somewhere In Time...................................$19.95	00694846 Testament – The Ritual $18.9
00692376 Cinderella – Long Cold Winter.................$18.95	00693095 Iron Maiden $22.95	00660084 Testament – Practice What You Preach ...$18.9
00692375 Cinderella – Night Songs $18.95	00694833 Billy Joel For Guitar $18.95	00694765 Testament – Souls Of Black $18.9
00694869 Eric Clapton – Unplugged........................$18.95	00660147 Eric Johnson Guitar Transcriptions.........$18.95	00694887 Thin Lizzy – The Best Of Thin Lizzy $18.9
00692392 Eric Clapton – Crossroads Vol. 1 ....$22.95	00694799 Robert Johnson – At The Crossroads $19.95	00694767 Trixter $18.9
00692393 Eric Clapton – Crossroads Vol. 2 ....$22.95	00660226 Judas Priest – Painkiller $18.95	00694410 The Best of U2...$18.9
00692394 Eric Clapton – Crossroads Vol. 3 ....$22.95	00693185 Judas Priest – Vintage Hits......................$18.95	00694411 U2 – The Joshua Tree...............................$18.9
00660139 Eric Clapton – Journeyman......................$18.95	00693186 Judas Priest – Metal Cuts........................$18.95	00660137 Steve Vai – Passion & Warfare ....$24.
00692391 The Best of Eric Clapton $18.95	00693187 Judas Priest – Ram It Down.....................$18.95	00694879 Stevie Ray Vaughan – In The Beginning ...$18.
00694896 John Mayall/Eric Clapton – Bluesbreakers..$18.95	00694764 Kentucky Headhunters –	00660136 Stevie Ray Vaughan – In Step $18
00694873 Eric Clapton – Timepieces.......................$18.95	Pickin' On Nashville.................................$18.95	00660058 Stevie Ray Vaughan –
00694788 Classic Rock $17.95	00694795 Kentucky Headhunters – Electric Barnyard.$18.95	Lightnin' Blues 1983 – 1987 ....$22.
00694793 Classic Rock Instrumentals......................$16.95	00660050 B. B. King $18.95	00694835 Stevie Ray Vaughan – The Sky Is Crying ..$18.
00694862 Contemporary Country Guitar $18.95	00660068 Kix – Blow My Fuse $18.95	00694776 Vaughan Brothers – Family Style............$18.
00660127 Alice Cooper – Trash $18.95	00694806 L.A. Guns – Hollywood Vampires.............$18.95	00660196 Vixen – Rev It Up ....$18.
00694840 Cream – Disraeli Gears $14.95	00694794 Best Of Los Lobos $18.95	00660054 W.A.S.P. – The Headless Children ....$18.
00694844 Def Leppard – Adrenalize $18.95	00660199 The Lynch Mob – Wicked Sensation $18.95	00694787 Warrant – Dirty Rotten Filthy Stinking Rich.$18.
00692440 Def Leppard – High 'N' Dry/Pyromania...$18.95	00693412 Lynyrd Skynyrd $18.95	00694866 Warrant – Dog Eat Dog...........................$18.
00692430 Def Leppard – Hysteria.............................$18.95	00660174 Yngwie Malmsteen – Eclipse....................$18.95	00694781 Warrant – Cherry Pie..............................$18.
00660186 Alex De Grassi Guitar Collection $16.95	00694845 Yngwie Malmsteen – Fire And Ice...........$18.95	00694786 Winger $18.9
00694831 Derek And The Dominos – Layla & Other	00694756 Yngwie Malmsteen – Marching Out $18.95	00694782 Winger – In The Heart Of The Young.......$18.
Assorted Love Songs $19.95	00694755 Yngwie Malmsteen's Rising Force $18.95	
00692240 Bo Diddley Guitar Solos..........................$18.95	00660001 Yngwie Malmsteen Rising Force – Odyssey.$18.95	
00660175 Dio – Lock Up The Wolves.......................$18.95	00694757 Yngwie Malmsteen – Trilogy....................$18.95	
00660178 Willie Dixon $24.95	00692880 Metal Madness $17.95	
00694800 FireHouse $18.95	00694792 Metal Church – The Human Factor $18.95	
00694867 FireHouse – Hold Your Fire.....................$18.95	00660229 Monster Metal Ballads $19.95	
00660184 Lita Ford – Stiletto $18.95	00694802 Gary Moore – Still Got The Blues............$18.95	